Ronald E. Henshaw

FEAR

FEAR

A POETIC SEQUENCE
concerning the loss of a child
and the search for redemption

by

Ronald E. Henshaw

WESTBOW°
PRESS
A DIVISION OF THOMAS NELSON
& ZONDERVAN

WestBow Press books may be ordered through booksellers or by contacting:

WestBow Press
A Division of Thomas Nelson & Zondervan
1663 Liberty Drive
Bloomington, IN 47403
www.westbowpress.com
1 (866) 928-1240

ISBN: 978-1-4908-2424-6 (sc)
ISBN: 978-1-4908-2425-3 (e)

Library of Congress Control Number: 2014902137

Printed in the United States of America.

WestBow Press rev. date: 02/04/2014

For my wife,
Linda McKnight Henshaw,
the most wonderful person that I have ever known.

Contents

Part I

the Tragedy

"As it was in the beginning...."

"....among **Fear's** long mountains...."

"Advent"
Haiku

When I began to....
When I learned to.... love....t'was then
I began to **fear**.

"Circles"

She had a flawless face, and fair, over-blown with her blond
      hair, down all about the shoulder, diaphanous the eyes, and
Blue, but elegant, not bold, her limbs long, the dream of Dance,
      the nightmare of Virtue, the perfect wave unwinding on my
Virgin shore of youth.

Songs we heard, oh, and sang them, every word. And then,
      among the after-wavelets, little ringlets, our love became like
Something satellites do swing upon, touching only as we passed,
      and at the last, released, she, moved on, to a farther star, thrusting,
Empty and bright.

But *my* circles did not wander from our world, and it was then
      I entered in, at one unknowing apogee, a mysterious atmosphere,
A nebulous terror whose black matrix is invisible forever, from
      whose dusky walls no light can shine, nor from whose **fear**some
Fold can life be free.

And so I called to her to come, to take from me the precious issue of
      our touching, circling far below, to wake him, to wrench him from his
Innocence. And I allowed for him to go. And I did pray that he forgive
      me, and that God would never let him know.... my shame. So it was,
He never knew.

Thus, in mortal union joined, quite unsound, my spirit uncommitted,
      the purest image of our touching I did *not*....**fear** to cast away. Yet,
We are the sum of *all* our circles, and our images remain wherever we
      have flown, beaming from that music, from that world which....cannot
Hold our circles.

Then they became a memory, but music as before, images of melodies
        we'll never sing again; *his* image, bringing to a stop. Remembrance and
Time, becoming that again which has not life. And our circles, parallel no
        longer, keep no bond between them but the image of an infant, ageless
For eternity.

Coming back now, the journey, the wonder, the wasted rending of the
        garment, spending thunder and lightning, ending in just that old, cold,
Falling, calling, recalling.... oh....with these I did
        circle the world.

"The Breaking of the Light"

I

When my soul moves, darkly,
Within the narrow well of Reason, it is....
My soul is.... like the palest vapor, palpating,
Pressing pallid fingers against the sterile
Stones of logic, probing, and ever I bow my head....
To the devils
Of despair.

II

When my soul moves, darkly,
Over seas of Self-pity, I wash myself in
Their black waters. I search the shore
For dim-lighted eyes that trust in tales
Contrived with lies. And I worship....
Weak words of
Sympathy.

III

When my soul moves, darkly,
Among **Fear's** long mountains, I seek no warm
Valleys deep, where the wind of the woods might
Sing aeolian symphonies, and my sorrowing soul
Might sleep. No I make my home on breathless peaks....
Or in caves of
Silent ice.

IV

My soul seems like the racing shadow of some cloud,
Bound for.... nothing.... but the breaking
Of the light.

"The Stone"
(a wife's confession)
a sonnet

We, as two vine branches
   weaving, have grown.
But aching between us, the
   coolness of stone.

Fear is the ruler of
   those who have known
Flowers of passion in
   gardens of stone.

Death is the harvest of
   seed that is flown
With a promise of life to a
   coffin of stone.

Your hopes were the wind, and as blindly have sown
   the seed of your love, and my heart is.... the stone.

"Early Morning"
(a husband's lament)

We awakened, he and I, lying still, in the quiet
Room, in a dark vacuum of newest morning.
Toys shimmered about the floor,
Vestiges of laughing yesterday, and
Before, portents of the day expected,
Memories, we assumed, of our
Tomorrows.

We listened, he and I, he was my son, we
Listened, selfishly, for sounds, for designs
Born of different ages, different places in time:
I, for the whisper of his breath, for my own
Heartbeat, an arrhythmic melody of **fear,** and,
Also, for the ringing remembrance of years;
He, for the movement of his mother, for the
Myriad stirrings of the morning, and, wishfully,
For the sounds of lover's voices, waking.
He is wiser than I,
Now.

Then the slant of light came in, a
Silent shot, misplaced, slicing the icy
Air thinly, like the edge of a thrown knife.
"When did you get up? I never know anymore.",
She, loveless.
"Mama", he breathed.
"I could not sleep. It is hard for me now.",
I, hopeless.
"Daddy", he whispered.
But his eyes closed, it was all right, no sense of
Impending doom, floating softly back to
Shantih for a while. And I am alone again,
Again, in the dawning light of our desert,
And no one there is to warn me, to speak
The thunder's words.

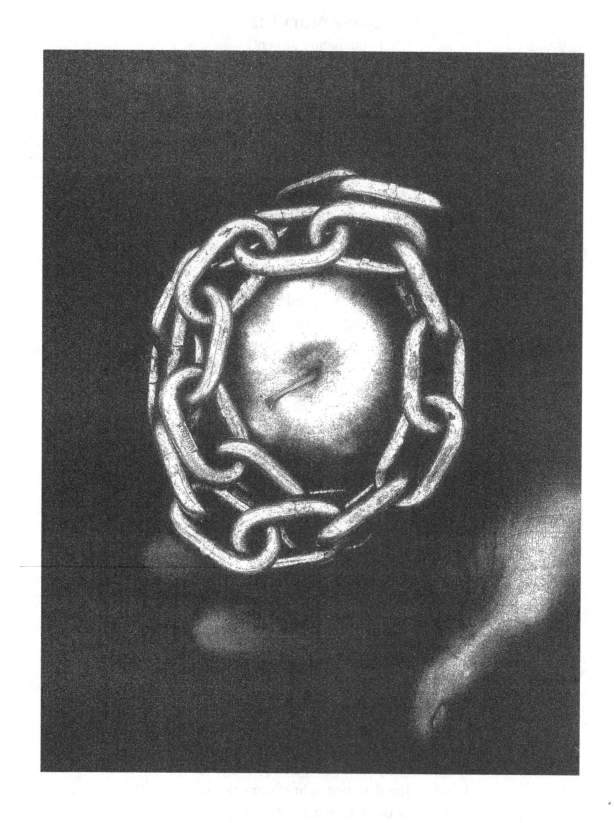

"Forbidden"
a sonnet

Could there be One, forbidden, by time and
Space, by fortune, **fear**, and circumstance,
Hidden forever by the light of the love of another,
Forbidden, oh...... to laugh, to dream, to dance
Together, to draw near without **fear**, to spend love,
To walk into tomorrow hand in hand, to bear sorrow
Heart to heart, and to hold hope for us within her?

Could there be One with which I'll never hear our
Tale of love be told, a bright blossom never to unfold?

Could there be One I'll look upon, concealing all true
Feeling, speaking words, yet silencing the heart?

Could there be One I warmly touch, then let depart?

Could there be One? There *is* but One,..... I know.....
Although..... eternally..... forever..... forbidden.

"The Open Sea"

We seem to stand, secretly touching,
     back to back, in the open sea.
I **fear** the pull of the spent waves of
     the past, you **fear** the deepness of
The rising tide of the future. So,
     we do not turn, do not embrace,
Rightly, in the calm of the present.
     Unsure of our strength not to fall
Beneath the ocean all around us,
     we seem to stand, secretly touching,
Back to back, in the open sea.

"Night. Ride. Home."

I

"Case number 868,299,
in the matter of the marriage...."

Uneasy rhythm.
Hum of wheels, slapping now and then,
Uneasy rhythm.
Your head, so sweet and heavy on
My thigh, your sanctuary,
Making the
Night.
Ride.
Home.

II

"....were legally married and lived
together as husband and wife...."

Such nights are like
Space that is *not* forever, with
Neon lightning, and plastic stars,
Electric constellations, and moons of
Sulphur, and amber pulsars flashing
Caution, caution, caution, caution.

III

"....they have had born to them
one (1) child....a boy...."

"Tell me a story, Daddy."
My thoughts wander in pastures of
Confusion. I have built my fences of
Doubt, and the eyes of panic watch from
Every dark corner. Oh keep....just keep
To the middle and dream of freedom.

IV

"....became insupportable....
discord and conflict....destroyed...."

"Once upon a time...."
I feel you sigh and stretch your
Little feet to touch the door.
I want to watch the contentment in
Your eyes, but if I do....you'll see the
Fear in mine.

V

"....dissolving the bonds of matrimony....
in the entitled and numbered cause....

Silver meadows press the road into
A fractured circle. But the road
It is that first attacked. The grass
Retaliates like the Armies of God.

VI

"Comes now the defendant....
waives....consents to the jurisdiction...."

There! In the glass!
Myself....my....face! What a
Wild spectre! It is reflection with
Reality beyond. But there is truth
In the transparency, and illusion in the
Reality, for the image remains, while
That which is around it.... changes.

22

VII

"....subject to reasonable visitation....
maintenance of said child...."

"Those stars look like a dragon."
"Where, Daddy?"
"Right there. The bright one is the eye."
"A dragon has fire in his mouth, Daddy."
"Well, you have to sort of pretend, like you
        do when I tell you stories, you have to imagine."
"I don't. Ever. I don't ever pretend."
"You don't?"
"No. I'm always afraid.... if I do.... I won't
"Come back...."

VIII

"....the said child....residing with the plaintiff....
        who is the fit and proper person...."

Your house is dark when we stop.
You rise up, still sleepy-eyed.
"Is Momma home?"
"Yes, Joe's there too."
As you pick up your grocery sack of toys
And clothes, your eyes ask,.... "why?...."
And my heart....cannot
Answer.

IX

"....at law and in equity."

Lights from the windows wash suddenly around us.
Distant waves of laughter, voices, break and
Drown you,.... and you are gone.
I. I, like a moccasin in dark water,
Retreat without a wake,
To make my
Night.
Ride.
Home.

"Eternal is the Night"
a sonnet

I dreamed we talked in love, last night,
     again, as long ago. We whispered sadness,
Laughter, hope, and **fear,** that we had shared, or
     wished we yet would come to know.

Again together we embarked on
     all our journeys bright. Again together
We did speak, as if immortal were our dreams,
     and eternal was the night.

Then waking in the hours after, gone again
     was all the laughter, spent the love,
Grown the **fear**, and though it seemed to reappear,
     lost the hope that we held dear.

And so, it seems, that mortal *are* the dreams
     we bring to life and light,.... and eternal *is* the night.

"Omen"

"My son amazes me
      the way that he puts life in things,
The way he conjures love from things
      not made of stuff of life and love."

(Can you not feel, can you not see
      that shadow, that dark beneath his door?
Can you not hear the whispering?)

"My son amazes me
      that he can see in us two beings
Worth the tender light upon his face,
      and tight to hold his precious hand."

(A rustling of the curtain as I enter,
      a movement in the mirror, a
Dark'ning of the window light....)

"My son amazes me,
      content to be with me, he brings
Much more to me than I to him."

(The silence as he slumbers coils around
      him like a shroud. I look at him in
Love and feel but **fear.)**

"As You Lay Down to Sleep"
(with my son, making shapes of the clouds on the day
before he was taken)

He who frees the captive breeze
  to wander o'er the Earth,
Has bound us all upon this ball
  of death and life and birth.
And weaving hot the Gordian knot
  our will with our devotions,
We seek some isle to lay awhile
  away these whirling motions.

Where warm's the ground and soft's the sound
  deep down in Autumn grasses,
Where by our feet, the Earth's blood-beat,
  a pearly river passes.
Where clouds are spun by wind and sun
  some old October day,
And we pretend each pattern spinned
  to be the ghost we may.

Where you and I can see the sky
  together, and the stream,
Where sunshine bright and starry night
  can circle while we dream.
Where one we are with moon afar,
  with folded silken sea,
With flight that swings on feathered wings,
  with circles in a tree,

Where we'll not hear the voice of **Fear,**
  nor see the shadow sweep
Across tomorrow with the sorrow
  that my heart will ever keep,
  as you lay down to sleep.

GARDEN OF THE INNOCENTS

THIS MY HEART
WELL UNDERSTANDS
THE CHILDREN ASLEEP
IN ALL GOD'S LANDS
ARE HOLY FLOWERS
IN ANGELS' HANDS.

"The Carpenter's Tools"
(at the grave of my son's step-father, on the east of The Garden of the Innocents)

I

(I, in the cemetery, you and he in your graves one week)

There are flowers in your bronze vase.
The ground above you is mounded and
New, but the pine needles hide your name.
The air caresses like fingers of the blind
Learning Braille. I feel as though I am some
One walking in the dark, early in the morning,
On tiptoe, with short breath, in a child's
Sleeping room. This is....a place to forgive,
Or....to suffer that which will not be forgiven.
These, shavings left from the working of the
Carpenter's Tools, the world swept clean, neatly
Done. You came between us and our bright
Endeavor, and then you fell to the floor in this
Pile of dust, and took, with you, our precious issue.
How I hated you.

(Smoke....I can walk, now, in, slow, circles,
all, round, you, in, smoke....
turn, you, up, side, down....smoke, curling
up from the soles of my feet.)

Which life is true life....if there is more than one?
For I feel lifeless here, as you are there, like the
Words from the lost man's bottle....cannot speak,
Only think, of the ship, the sail, white, and smoothe
Like a baby's brain....but no "discovery" unfolds
Itself for me; like a fetus in a gigantic womb, in a
New nation, among citizens who speak, but do
Not answer in their repose; before me, yet behind
Me, above me, yet below me, graceful as gravity,
Invisible as time. Why did you go? Where are you
Now? And why were *you* ordained to don Sisyphean
Robes in the presence of he who was mine?
And why did I hate you so?

31

Oh. Yes. I remember. When I was weak, when I
Failed, when I was confused, when I was alone,
And when I wept for all these things, that was when
I hated you.

And when I left my son at your door every Sunday
Night for years, breaking his brand, new, heart.
You comforted him, made it all better, wanted
Him for your own, and his embraces, meant for me,
Belonged to you. That was when
I hated you.

And then, once, we stood in the yard with him,
And as I left, I said, "Give your Daddy a kiss,"
And he went to you. That was when
I hated you.

And he spoke of you, the builder of his home, the
The hunter, you, like a pirate king who lived with
My wife in the eyes of my son. That was when
I hated you.

Oh, yes, but I felt them! Coming down! I felt them!
Coming down on you and he! And I just had time to
Draw back my hand when she called one night and
Said, "They are dead." "Why?" I asked, not how,
Or when, but, "Why?" Oh, yes, I remember, it was.....
The Carpenter's Tools.

II

(I, in the cemetery, you and he in your graves one year)

There are no flowers in your bronze vase,
And the ground above you is sinking.
The pine needles still hide your name.
The vapors are melting in the illness of
The day. Upwards, in the tall trees, a rising
Fever of warm wind spreads it's fingers
Through the old men's thinning hair, saying
"Go!" The pines draw their life from the
Very fertile soil below, dropping their intentions
Of immortality on your mortal home, all the
While reaching for the mirage of the sky.
So, now, the Carpenter's Tools have lain you
Down like a tall pine tree, have answered your
Prayers, fulfilled your dreams, the Langoliers
Have done their work, and the shop, still clean,
Hums with the mighty continuum.

(Smoke....right, side, up, now, cool smoke....
like from hot ice, early in the winter grass smoke,
curling up around my head smoke, silent smoke,
after the whispered winnowing of....
The Carpenter's Tools.)

It has been (so soon!) a year now.
Still, I am weak. Still, I fail. I am even more
Alone. And I have fallen beyond confusion.
But....it was *you* that I hated so.

As I pick the petals from the flowers in the
Bronze vases that surround us, I cannot help
But see that something....something that
Hates a wall and cracks a road and covers a
Shrine all over with sand, threatens to devour
The tarnished plaques as they cry out!....
"Together Forever", "Forever Beloved"
Never Forgotten", echoes of Ozymandias.

Oh, it is so dark for the living when the embers
That burn us now and then turn cold. My
Companion wanders toward me. "Come,
Let us go. It is time. "Yes, it is time. Watch!
Draw back *your* hand. For I **fear** the darkness,
And I feel the nearness of....
The Carpenter's Tools.

"Absalom"

It hurts me so badly to have you gone
       when I loved you so much,
Oh my son.

My life is so lonely without your sweet voice
       to hear in the morning,
Oh my son.

Not to reach and touch your hand,
       nor feel your small embrace,
Nor lie beside you while you sleep,
       and look upon your face,
Dims the light of dawn and dulls
       the sharpness of the night,
And takes me down to Hell as deep
       as Heaven at it's height.

My heart is so empty, my eyes are so blind,
       my hand, so unfeeling and cold,
My step, so uncertain, my mind, so unsound,
       my spirit, unspeakably old.
Will you know that I loved you, that the years
       fell to ruin when I let the insidious
Tyrant of **Fear** compel me to enter his fold?

Oh my son, my son....
       oh Absalom, my son.

"A Natural Thing"

I dreamed of you last night, my son,
    but you were changed, all dark and different
Than when we were young.

I stood alone at night, my son,
    before a forest, and the mist was white,
Rolling in the air.

And then your image formed, my son,
    from the smoke, and you began to walk to
Me, as you did once.

You had become a man, my son,
    while I had grown no older. From your eyes
Shone....no light of life.

But when you spoke to me, my son,
    it was the voice that I recalled, your young
Voice of days long dead.

"Where have you been these years, Father,
    and why did you leave me here? I have been
Waiting." Yes, I know.

I told another about my dream, about your face,
    about the empty place I made.
She said it was a natural thing, that I should have
    no **fear**....she said it was....
A natural thing....and I should have no **fear**.

"The Shattered Mirror"

a sonnet

Standing astride the shattered mirror, I,
      the Collossus of **Fear**, invader of Lilliput,
Regard the shards at my feet, glittering shards,
      staring up with the terrible eye of the fly.

I cannot recall their week of creation,
      their advent, or the age of their evolution.
I cannot remember the day of their fall,
      I cannot imagine their blest absolution,

To be one as they were, to reflect again
      one face of their maker. In them all
I can only hear clearly that each small mirror,
      scattered, speaks a secret of a shattered soul.

And I wonder, was my image ever clearer?
      Were the pieces ever whole?

"Solitude"

a sonnet

Holy sanctuary sweet,
      bless'ed solitude complete,
As the snowy white of silence
      at the Pole,

Where the glaring eyes of **Fear**
      in the glass will not appear,
And my steps out in the sun
      will not control,

Where the mountains of the mind,
      under forests, unconfined,
Feed their rivers to the ocean
      of the soul.

(Yet the sea will rise to rain....
      and descend into the mountains once again.)

"Cold Front"
Haiku

Hands against the wind.
Turned head. Eyes tight shut. **Fear** hits.
Icy blue Norther.

"Time and the Wind"
a sonnet

We are the foster children of Time,
     we are the step-brothers of the Wind.
These are the guardians of the flesh,
     not of the mind.

We are the foundlings of the Earth,
     nursed in the cradle of days that end.
We are the wards given to those
     not of our kind.

Time is the keeper of the gate;
     a faithful soul, the Wind will hate.
Time and the Wind are lover's, wild,
     and **Fear** is their bastard child.

From our shepherds I'll soon be free,
     asleep in the arms of the Lotus tree.

"The Lotus Tree"
a sonnet

With the flower of the lotus, in the hour
      of the night, I take communion of the host.
Heavy lashes lay the ashes of my daydreams
      on the light. Gone again my grinning ghost.

My escaping of the raping of my life by
      fear again, drives me deeper to the wood.
No one follows through the hollows of the forests
      of the brain. No one follows. No one could.

At the portal, on the bound'ry of the mortal
      universe, in the shadow of the leaf,
Shall I sever **fear** forever, free the spirit
      from the curse, and lift the burden of the grief?

Carve a coffin of this tree
      that so sweetly shelters me.

"The Beast"

Fear is a beast, the Beast,
　　　prolonging night as it feeds,
Unreasoning, no reason for it
　　　to be here, again.

Feast upon my flesh, beast, and I
　　　will crumble in your mouth, a clod
Of dust, choking you, for I am
　　　nothing, and the victory is mine.

"Nightmare"

Nightmare crept in, so silently and sweet,
        a dream, a jewel of the night, to keep.
It then began to change....like cold, wet
        pictures painted on the mists of sleep,
Like scenes through water on a window pane,
        like pages of my past written in the rain.
Toward morning it had drained down to the
        secret dungeons of my brain.

The bowman calmed his aim, recalling ancient
        law. The prey was weak and **fear**ful of the
Wood, and it began to claw, to molt, to
        shed the outer skin, to break the bond of
Evil unto Good. And then it watched, without
        hope, the bowman's draw. And I, the
Bowman, pitied not the prey, it's face I never
        saw. And so then I....I let the arrow fly.

And when it struck, all disappeared, the
        prey, the bow, the arrow, and the wood.
But then....*I* felt the pain....*mine* was the scream....
        I held the **fear** as the terror of the dream
Came clear: that when I let the arrow fly to rid my
        soul of it's dark side....it is now *I* shall die!

It shot from out *my* mouth, the cry, and from *my*
        heart, the pain, and t'was *my* mind that filled with
Fear....when I beheld what spilled.... upon the ground
        t'was *my* own blood, the spreading of the stain.

"Parasite"
Haiku

Fear feeds from my bowl
Of guilt, self-doubt; consumes, it
Seems, even my soul.

"Black"
Haiku

Night, jet black, hard cold,
Star, bright, wind, still, sound, flat, dead,
Feed my **fear** to die.

"Eyes"
Haiku

I saw she had no
Eyes. "**Fear** not," said she, "neither
Do *I* see *your* eyes."

"The Sum of All My Seasons"

I

My arrogant youth dripped disgust for the
    rich, red wine which it arose in, lightly,
Blindly, like a bubble. And late in Spring,
    leaping at the surface, freely, silently
Blew itself apart.

II

And then my prime, the Summer of my time,
    I spent with spinning in the air, climbing on
The clouds above, caring not enough to love
    the home my heart would land in, as the
Season dropped me down.

III

The wind of anxious age is blowing 'cross the
    fallow field I fell in, the glowing of the
Sun has now begun, and I, with lips and arms
    of a lonely lover, embrace the meadow,
Late, late, in Autumn.

IV

As Winter waits, I see no paths, no ways to
    walk in. Wisdom has not gone before
Me, nor has love pursued me. Neither have I
    sought. I feel that only **fear** will be
The sum of all my seasons.

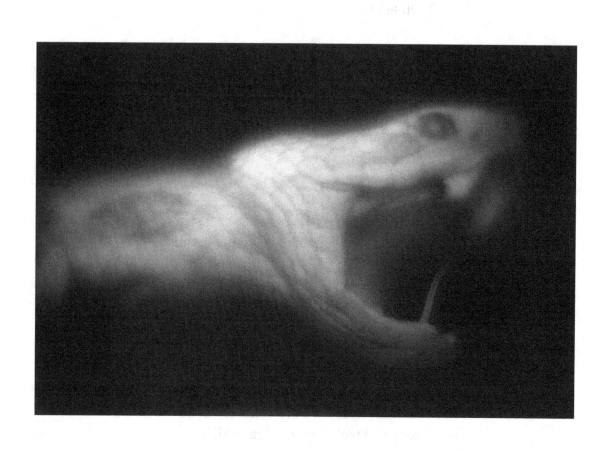

"Fear"
a villanelle

My sun went down in my early light.
My blood grows thin, my will grows weak.
So cold is the mouth of the parasite.

I do not think I see things right.
I do not find, although I seek.
My sun went down in my early light.

My body screams of cold at night,
And then remembers not the chill.
So cold is the mouth of the parasite.

What feeds on me, his eyes grow bright.
My eyes grow dim, he takes my will.
My sun went down in my early light.

Come, then, sun, to me, again with light,
To be the hunter who makes the kill,
So cold is the mouth of the parasite,

To set me free from **fear** and flight,
To answer, answer, why I write,
"My sun went down in my early light,
So cold is the mouth of the parasite".

Part II

Epiphany

"....is now, and ever shall be...."

"....If Chance would set this world in motion,
wherefore then arise devotion...."

"Dawn"
Haiku

Fear not the dawn. Rings
Of smoke drift where darkness burned,
Blown out by the Light.

"The Center of the Circle"

I

There is....Mind....and the thought there is, and then the
Whimper....and the atom....of light....splits....and the
Mass appears, boiling, roaring, rushing outward,
Consuming emptiness, and the speed, imponderable,
And the movement, the movement, all within and without,
The same at all levels, and then the Circle forms, and in it
Many circles, and in them all is heat and light and sound and
Fury, and nothing is love nor **fear** nor hate nor pain nor
Joy nor any further thought beyond the first, inside the
Circle.
But what is....at the center of the Circle....? What is....
What is....no, not at the center of the Circle....what is....
Who is....standing back from the Circle, watching....?

II

After all, whence came the thought? And what, who, will
Remain when the Circle breaks, and the heat and the light
Fade, blink out, and the sound and the fury subside, and
All comes rushing back unto itself, slowly, then faster,
Faster, faster, and the mass unto the atom, and the atom,
Whole again, unto the whimper, and the whimper unto the
Thought, and the thought unto the
Mind?
What....who....will step into the void, into the smoke,
And wave it all away, and sit, and ponder....alone....
Omniscient....stroking the sidereal beard....wondering....
Wondering.... What was it that was not there....not there?
And then it will all begin again.... Mind will bear the
Thought....the thought will cry the whimper.... the
Whimper becomes the atom....of light....and splits....unto
The mass.... boiling, roaring....and the mass will form the
Circle....but this time....
This time....

III

They will all be there....all....inside....at
            The Center of the Circle.

"The Sixth Day"
(the evolution of Creation)

Wherefore, then, and when, came that great divide,
     that unbreachable chasm, endless, limitless, fathomless,
Between the smallest and grandest of beasts and creatures,
     between them all, and every manner of man?

That man was one of them, one among them all, as one
     with them since that day, the first day, when Energy
Itself obeyed the grand command and leapt across it's
     own equation, condensing, concentrating, forming
Circle after circle, into mass and matter, that he *was* one
     among creatures, no more than the mammoth, no less
Than the atom, that he *was* them, as they were he,
     of this.....there can be no doubt.....

Until that day, the fifth day, turned to fabulous night, and
     he lay with them, and slept with them, and dreamed their
Dreams with them, until that night, that hour, that second,
     Until the *now* of timeless eternity, when Spirit went
Flowing into the forests of the world, in search of the man,
     found him, lay with him, loved him, entered him, gave
Light to the Man, forever dividing Him from the beasts and
     creatures, granting to Him the crown of Creation, planting
In Him the seed of the Soul, revealing to Him the design of the
     infinite Life, the **fear** of the infinite Death, lashing His body
With the bondage of Time, binding His mind to the burden
     of Guilt and Shame, to the knowledge of Good and Evil,
Of this.....there can be no doubt.....

And, so, *therefore*, then, came that great abyss, the eternal
     divide, unbreachable forever, endless, limitless,
Fathomless, between the smallest and grandest of beasts,
     between them all and every manner of Man, so, that, when
again the sun caressed all flesh, that morn, the sixth day, He
     awakened, aware of His being, and whispered, "I *am*.",
Of *This*,..... there can be no doubt.

73

"The Gift"
Israel
(Hosea 11:1-11)

I fashioned for myself a child, and
      a countenance I gave to him
Like unto a portrait in the sunlight,
      but in his darkness and unfounded
Dread, he turned his face away from Me.

With intellect and sensuous perception did
      I fill his mind, in the image of My own,
But greater value did he place upon the
      ignorance of men, and greater joy did
He take in the blindness of his sin.

I gave to him a steady hand, and strong,
      which he did raise to Me in arrogance
And wrath. His feet I made to move as
      one with majesty and song, but then he
Ran so fast away, so far, that he was lost.

Yet, one day, as I wandered in the forests
      of the world, I knew his face again, and
Again he turned away. But then I reached
      and put My hand upon his cheek, and I
Turned his head to Me, and I met his eyes.

The golden countenance was gone, the eyes
      were filled with **fear**, the strong hands
Trembled, and the feet were red with blood.
      He raised his hand to Me again, but when it
Opened, there in it was a gift, to Me, a figure,
      an image of himself that he had made. And
So I drew him near, and from his feet I washed
      the blood, and from his eyes, the **fear**, and
I did still his trembling hands, and I did take
      him home again, with Me.

"Blue Asylum"

(after <u>The Unexpected Universe</u> by Loren Eiseley)

I

I watch insane clouds in a blue asylum,
Insane clouds, with tucked tails and
Bowed heads, follow in crowds the
Maniacal wind, insane clouds all wrapped
In gray shrouds, confined in the blue asylum.

II

Mind is a blue asylum, full of day, full of night,
Full of clouds, gray and white, full of dark,
Full of light, full of cold, full of heat, full of
Fair winds and frantic storms, and full of **fear**
For when the blue asylum turns to black.

III

I see the Earth, like an altar, where the
Ancient light leaps and falters from new
Candles and old, the ancient light passed to
Our tapers at behest of the Priest, one after
One, by the touch of the acolyte. Though the
Flame grows, the tallow melts, and I consider
That, if I choose, I may darken my light, now,
With a single easy breath upon it. But then....
I am startled by something .... that
I cannot see.

IV

The philosopher says,
"I observe a hopeless defense: a lizard frozen in
The gleam of the eye of the cat. But, neither hunter
Nor hunted, I AM that which, I AM, that which
They cannot see.
And as I toss the stone between lizard, cat,
They are moved by the hand.... that
They cannot see."

V

The philosopher says,
"I consider the spider, weaving it's web of
Symmetrical beauty, (not beauty to him,
But to me). He senses and sees the stick
That strokes, that halts the spinning defining
All spiders, but not the hand that wields the
Stick, nor the will that wields the brain. I throw
Not a shadow on the island of Spider, but he is
A rider with me. He is moved by the hand.... that
He cannot see."

VI

Mind is the hunter as well as the hunted,
No weapon but the will, no defense but flight
From that which it can feel but cannot see.
Mind is an artist, a consummate weaver of illusion,
Casting thread after thread across the blue asylum,
Until we have our web to walk upon, back and forth,
Avoiding severed strands, seizing, binding, poisoning,
Consuming our venom as well as our captive, and ever
Pursuing a new vibration. That vibration! What
Touched my web? Am *I* a part of something.... that
I cannot see?

VII

So, like a lizard I sit, frozen in the gleam of the
Eye of death. So, like a cat I run, **fear**ing the
Strike of the unexpected. So, like a spider I cling
To my web, drawn tight 'cross the azure abyss.
Four living creatures in the wheel within the wheel,
All in a blue asylum, all a part of something.... that
They cannot see.

"self"
Haiku
(after "A man feared..." - Stephen Crane-
an opposing view)

Two men walk the woods
One **fear**'s an assassin, one
fear's it is he. Fools.

"The River"

In a dream, I was young, I swam in a
Swift river that was clear and black from
The images of thick trees on it's banks.
The river was the sweetest, coolest water,
And I drank of it until I was heavy and cold
Inside. But then I looked around, and I was
Alone. Everyone had climbed out before me,
And there was no place for me to get out.
I became afraid of the grassy banks of the
River. The water had begun to recede, and
I could see under the banks where it was dark,
And the roots of the trees hung down like hair
Into the water, and the banks became higher
And higher, and my **fear** of them grew inside me.
I swam to the middle of the river where it was
Deep, and I went under. When I came up again
I swam for the banks that I was afraid of. I
Became afraid of the river. I **fear**ed the shore.
The river dropped lower and lower, and the banks
Rose higher and strange to me. But I had to get out
Or I would drown. There was one branch that I
Could reach. If I could catch it and hang on, I would
Climb out into the sun. But if I reached for it,
I would have to stop swimming, and if I missed
It, I would drown. It came closer and closer. I
Stopped swimming and reached with all my
Strength....
But the river still goes on and on....
Down to the sea.

"Golgotha"

(Christ on the cross with the thieves,
and, perhaps, His thoughts.)

a sonnet

I long to be with raisins fed,
    refreshed with apples, cool and red.
My heart, it weakens, ill with love
    for those below, for Him above.
My sight, with death, grows dim and dull
    but bless'ed sees no more "the Skull".

(He hungers for the pleasures of the Earth.)

(He feels the frailty of His humanity.)

In anger Israel has decried Us,
    We feel the **fear** of those beside Us.
But we shall hold their horrid hands,
    so when we trod untroubled lands
Together, We shall walk upon
    the water through eternal dawn.

(As He joins the Trinity, He begins to think as three persons.)

Abba, Abba! Eli, Eli!....lama....lama sabachthani!
    Father....Father, I am....cold. Father...I AM....

(He calls to the Father.)
(He gives up his Spirit.)

"Energy Levels"
Haiku

Love, the knowledge of
the beauty of Being; **Fear**,
the knowledge of not.

"Ode to Life"

Liquid Life, forever flowing
Through our universe unknowing,
Will the seed within you growing
Flower from the roots of Man?

With your throbbing undulation,
Secret source, and destination,
Has a God in self-creation
Set your purpose and your plan?

Is the voice within my mind
The Infant God within mankind
Commanding of Himself to find
His way across your span?

Long have we, in deep reflection,
Sought to hold some vague direction;
If our souls should find perfection,
Would this be the death of Man?

If in the womb of life on Earth,
Our souls should die before rebirth,
Would we alone have will or worth,
Or would *this* be the death of Man?

If Chance would set this world in motion,
Wherefore, then, arise Devotion,
Love, and Hate, and **Fear**, the ocean
Measureless, the mind of Man?

In the time that you course through me,
If the questions that pursue me
Light the paths of Truth unto me.....
Let me walk them where I can.

"Time"
Haiku

Time is illusion,
bondage. **Fear** to wander there.
Now is eternal.

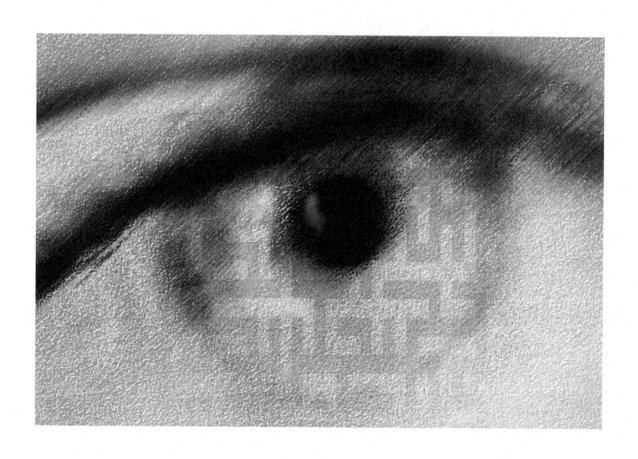

"The Fires of Time"

I

Minutes, minutes, measured slowly,
     as for evil, as for holy,
Softly, softly, runs the rhyme,
     tinder to the Fires of Time.

There is a closet in the hall,
     where something lonely seems to call.
Another's will I can't ignore
     compels me to the shuttered door.

Then falling fast from out my hand,
     the open door reveals a band
Of faded blossoms, barren seeds,
     now even plucked from mem'ries weeds.

And though I feel I may intrude
     upon this mournful interlude,
I know I come not unexpected,
     for I've been by them collected.

Something softly shuts me in it,
     in a dark, eternal minute,
Here I feel my heartbeat, breath,
     and sense the after-flow of death.

But then, a faint light, slowly rising
     like the moon, not recognizing
All the shapes of sun-lit Earth,
     now bears them gentle, warm rebirth.

And glancing round the room I find
     things living only in God's mind,
For mortal mem'ry's made to hold
     no still-born child, no tale untold.

Scenes upon the road not taken,
        promises now long forsaken,
Lie in waste and wait to prime
        the never-failing Fires of Time.

II

But still I hear a faint voice falling
        soft upon my mind and calling
Me to come and draw at last
        the heavy curtain of the past.

Deeper down the void I'm drawn,
        though my heart pounds, my **fear** is gone.
And kneeling in this cold, dead place,
        I sense a warm and living grace.

Suspended in a cloudy cream
        of silence round my self I dream,
I feel, not life nor death herein,
        but cinders where the two have been.

There, in the corner, caught forever,
        by a moment changing never,
My father's eyes return my gaze
        from long ago forgotten days.

A photograph upon the floor,
        a vision of what is no more,
A kitten and a little boy,
        a moment time did not destroy.

Did you remain the long years through,
        just as that moment captured you?
And did you smile the minutes after?
        or did sorrow drown your laughter?

Where did Life's long seasons take you?
        Where did Life at last forsake you?
Did you stem with vict'ry, pride,
        your sea of shame, your failure's tide?

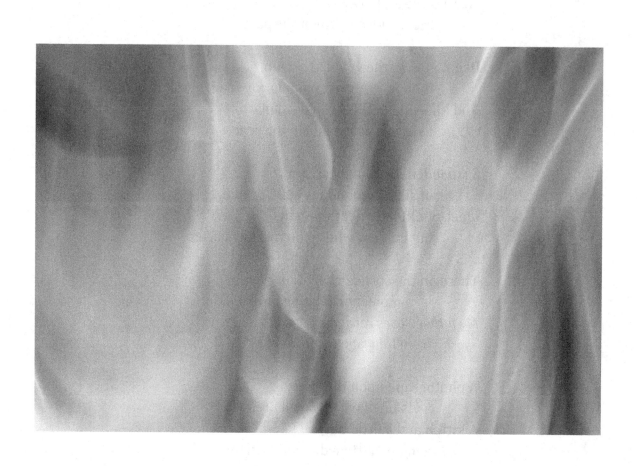

Someone looked into your eyes
      and dreamed a dream for you that flies
Like smoke and ashes blow and climb
      above the raging Fires of Time.

III

With trembling hands I hold these two,
      and place them on the shelf for you,
That you may look in love and **fear**
      if e'er you chance to enter here.

The ancient photograph my lose
      the color of the buckled shoes,
The ruffled shirt, the tassled hat,
      the stripes upon the little cat,

But there was then a youthful smile
      upon my father's face a while,
And it will always be a part
      of God's own great, eternal heart.

And so Life's mysteries are made,
      that such a moment in the shade
Of many greater moments blended,
      once begotten, ne'er is ended.

Minutes, minutes, measured slowly,
      as for evil, as for holy,
Softly, softly, runs the rhyme,
      tinder to the Fires of Time,
To the demon Fires of Time.

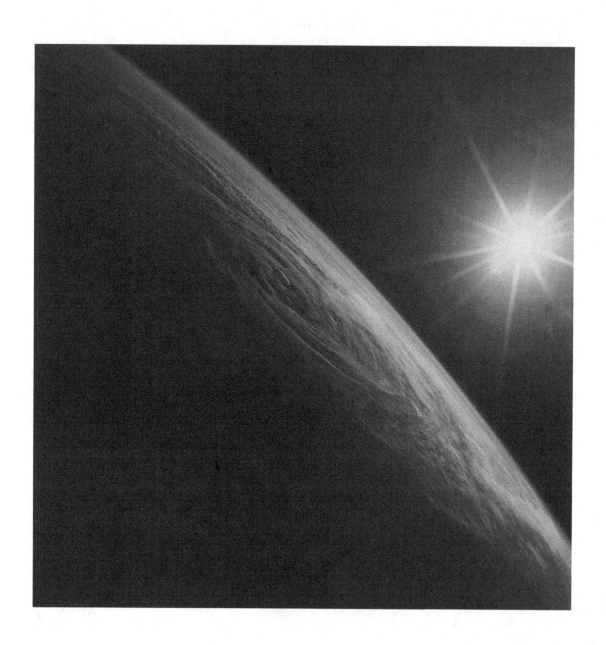

"On the Day of the End of Time"
an oracle

(The day on which Time itself shall cease to be, and the
Earth and all the Life therein shall become eternal.)

I
On the eve of the day of the end of Time,
To the hours just before the dawn,
The muted melody of starlight will
Dissolve into darkness.
The tumultuous tuning of the
Instruments of the Cosmos will cease.
A stillness will abide. The baton will tap.
And the embryonic eyes of Earth will turn
To the fading lunar light, in **fear** to the fading light.

II
The concert of the Universe will begin
It's unending crescendo.

III
All of the colors contained in the spectrum
Will flash to their final degree. They will
Fuse to form a new white light that will dawn
On the day of the end of Time, caressing the
Flesh of the Earth forever. A ring, like unto a
Rainbow, will begin to encircle the world.

IV
The engine in a cloud will rise to
His maximum revolutions.

V

The scent of Heaven and the smoke of Hell
Will seep through the bound'ries of all their
Dimensions to meld with the moisture of Earth. The
Mirrored walls will fall. The curtains will be cut,
Recalling the veil at the Crucifixion, confirming the
Letter to Corinth. The fountains of Heaven and the
Forests of Hell will be seen as the same as the Earth.

VI

The sum of the number of every dimension
will be counted as only nine.

VII

At the turn of the Tarot card,
 the mask of the Healer will melt,
Revealing the face, and sealing the fate,
 of the dealer in death,
Who'll be dealt Her own reward.
The Cup will be found in the Ark.
The Light will eliminate dark.
The Earth will be equal to Heaven and Hell.
The circle will close with a spark.

VIII

The Riddle will run to rhythm and rhyme....
 on the day of the end of Time.

"Arabesque"

I

"Tell me the equation."
"Life is the Energy."
"Yes...."
"Death is the equal sign."
"But what of the....
Other side?"
"I have given you Reason,
Wrapped it in Hope. I have
Tied them with the ribbons of
Time. A unique gift."
"This end to things! It
Confounds my Reason!"
"It will be so. But cast away
The ribbon, tear not the wrapping,
Honor the gift."
"You are a phantom!"
"I am The Infant."
"Can you solve the Equation
For me?"
"No. If you doubt my purpose, how
Can you believe, or even hear, the
Things that I would tell you? I will
Give life to you, and I will ask
Death with my eternal voice, but
You, you must search naked in the
Holy, mortal darkness, and with
My gift, *you* must find the answer."
"But..... I am
Afraid."

II

Three kings, diverse, upon the road,
yet singular the goal,
They wield the ancient tools with which
to shape the final soul.

The first, conceived in battle,
holds a sword above his head.
The last, he moves in spirit to
the living from the dead.

The one between the two,
he throws no shadow of his own,
But rides the road in **fear** and shame,
bewildered and alone.

And he is twisted round the knot
of life and death and birth,
While God defines his image in
the mirror of the Earth.

III

"Listen!
I will give to him peace,
Dissolve all his struggles, and
Soothe his cuts. I will break the
Circles for you. I will soften the
Rocks beneath your feet. He
Bends the high weeds on the
Unknown plain, and you, you
Must overtake him. I will melt
His sabre into milk. I will give
You freedom from the need for
Sustenance of the flesh. He will
Carve a story in Braille, and you
Must learn to read it with the
Fingers of your
Reason...."

105

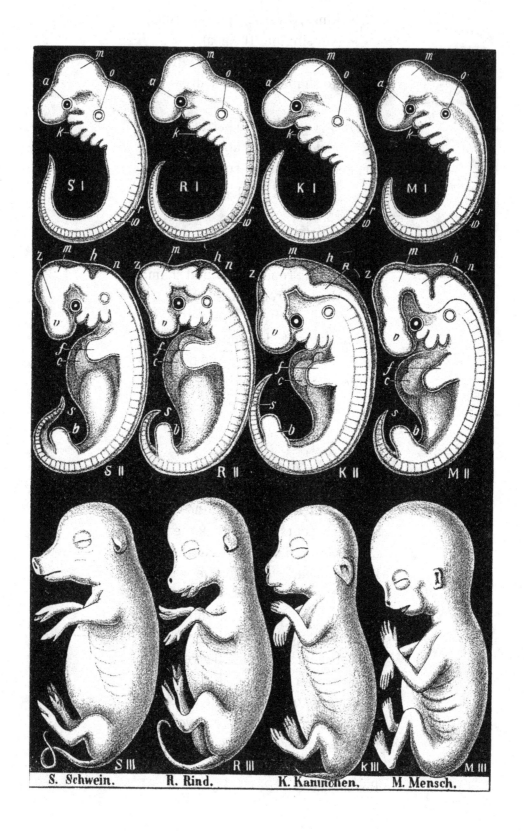

S. Schwein. R. Rind. K. Kaninchen. M. Mensch.

IV

Three portraits hang upon a wall
    of Time and Earth and Space,
And one is cloudy, incomplete,
    yet flawless through the face.

And one grows dimmer with each stroke
    that finishes the first,
The one between now ebbs and flows,
    And cries his fate be cursed.

The one it takes the softness of
    the moon upon the rise,
The other grim as granite in
    the fading of the eyes.

The one between the two is blind,
    and floats within the frame,
He feels but **fear** and loneliness
    and longs to know his name.

V

"Truly, I say unto you,
Do not be anxious about
Your rise and your fall,
For when I call you, you will
Know your name. You are all
Made by the thoughts of my mind.
I have fashioned you, and by your
Hand and mind, you will bear me!
I have created laws, and I will exist
Within them! Not one is broken that
Does not hinder me, the Infant, but like
The scar, increases my strength. Find and
Trace the laws with the flashes of
Your reason....and I will live!
unto my creation...."

VI

Three candles burning in the dark,
     they warm the common seed.
From each to each the wick is run
     to nurse the Infant's need.

The first floats o'er a melted pool,
     yet flickers not the fire.
The second falters like regret,
     then flashes like desire.

The third, it pulls the purpose
     And the steady light from one,
And from the other gathers in
     the brilliance of the sun.

The tallow is a broader mold,
     as if to burn the longer,
And with the fading of the two,
     it's flame is ever stronger.

VII

How strange to be so quickly old
     when all before was youth,
To trace the aimless arabesque
     that seemed a search for Truth.

"....I was found by those who
     did not seek me...."

There was no end itself I saw
     that drew the pale design,
But only finding no escape
     that wrote the loop and line.

"....through knowledge....
     comes escape...."

110

How dark the night of younger days,
      how bright the break of dawn,
What irony at last to see
      the way that's all but gone.

"....prepare the way....
      before me...."

My **fear** was that the road I ran
      would never lead to light,
But now I **fear** the setting sun,
      the certainty of night.

"....**fear** not....
      for I am with you...."

How dear I hold companions
      now I know the stay is brief,
And feel much wilder winds of joy
      above the clouds of grief.

"....I have come to give you life....
      abundantly...."

And it must be the sweeter sigh,
      the last, long, throbbing breath,
For nothing save the mind of Man
      so dwells in dreams of death.

"....O death, where is thy sting....
      O grave, where is thy victory...."

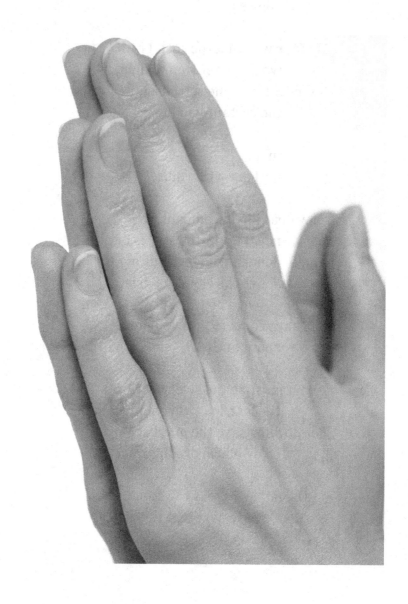

"Essence"

Where there is pure heat,
    there can be no cold,
Where there is pure light,
    there can be no dark,
Where there is pure love,
    there can be no hate,
Where there is pure faith,
    there can be no **fear**.

"Reconciliation"

These things had I prayed for
      he who was lost. As for those that
May follow, bearing his blood, I pray
"In the name of the Father...."
Let them give
      without taking,
Let them take
      without grieving,
Let them see
      without searching,
Let them hear
      without speaking,
      "....and of the Son...."
Let them speak
      without whisp'ring,
Let them feel
      without touching,
Let them think
      without **fear**ing,
Let them hope
      without doubting,
      "....and of the Holy Spirit...."
Let them rest
      without dying,
Let them live
      without hurting,
Let them love
      without needing,
And be loved
      without changing.

Lord, may any one, or many, or
      even none, be Thy will,
Let it be.

"The Lonely Heart"
Haiku

To feed the lonely
Heart will never fill the heart
With love, only **fear**.

"For Love to Come"
a sonnet

There, behind the **fear**ful gate
   unto your heart, I know you wait,
As always, even now so late,
   for love to come.

Deep sorrow for a dream that's died,
   in your contempt you cannot hide,
And you'll not lay to rest your pride,
   'till love has come.

Beyond the gate you never thought
   to go. But love must e'er be sought,
And love, *with* love, must e'er be bought,
   for love to come.

Time soon will end our contemplating. You must end your hesitating.
   Lonely is your love, long waiting, just for *you* to come.

"One"
a sonnet

O have you come to me,
      come to me at last,
One not in passion, nor with longing,
      nor in **fear** of night's despair,
One not to bless, one not to borrow,
      not in rapture, nor in sorrow,
One not with ears that hear the past,
      one not with eyes that seek tomorrow,
One not with promises to keep,
      one not with bitter woe to bear,
Have you come to me at last,
      O have you come to me,

Just to be....but One with me....
      for what we ask in prayer?

"Love Is"
a sonnet

Wanting is but a quiet and feeble Greed,
      yet has no small respect for Need.
And Wishing's hope without Desire,
      like Dreams are smoke that has no Fire.

But Love! Love is the Crown of our Creation,
      Love is the Engine of Salvation,
Love is the Queen of Life, and all the Living,
      the Grandest Gift of all our Giving.

Love speaks to us with softest, lyric voice,
      and offers one exquisite choice:
Be silent, turn away, neither laugh, neither cry,
      neither seek to live, nor rightly, truly, *fear* to die;

Or turn, and draw Love near, embrace, enfold, and sigh,
      and with your *Life*.....reply.

"These Abide"
Haiku
(1 Corinthians 13:13)

Should light of Truth blind
Reason, *Faith, Hope* blind **fear;** *Love*
lights eternity.

"I pray my long poem....."

I pray my long poem at last to be done.
      I pray I have gathered the fairest of all
The petals I've lost into one.
      I pray my long poem be done.

I pray my long poem have intricate rhyme.
      I pray when the day that my poem is heard,
That music will fly out of every word.
      I pray my long poem to rhyme.

I pray my long poem is read by the world.
      I pray that each phrase will turn darkness to light,
And that **fear** unto faith is unfurled.
      My long poem I give to the world.

I pray my long poem to peacefully end,
      and when it is read by my Saviour and Friend,
May all of the syllables beautifully blend.
      I pray my long poem to end.

I pray my long poem is born once again,
      through the fountains of Heaven, washed of all sin,
Embraced by my Lord, a work worthy of men.
      I pray to be born again,
My long life to be born again.

"Exit Music"
a sonnet

When the silken pillow's placed
      at last beneath my head,
And I lay down, embroidered, laced
      with filigree and thread,
When faith and hope have been replaced,
      and I am drained of all my dread,
Must I remember how obsessed
      with **fear** was I, how dark with doubt?
Must I recount each sin confessed,
      forbidden thought, each wayward route?
Must I recant each ill behest,
      must I *relive* what Heaven lives without?

Must I descant, descant, on my shame....?
      (Or may I offer but my name?)

"Epitaph"

He thought too much, and much too oft,
    about the things one cannot touch.
His thoughts and **fear**s, not wings
    that hold aloft the birds, but things
That hold aloft the wings.

"The Answer"
Haiku

To the question of.....
What force frees this world from **Fear?"**
The answer is.....

(one Word, in this book)

"....world without end,
amen."